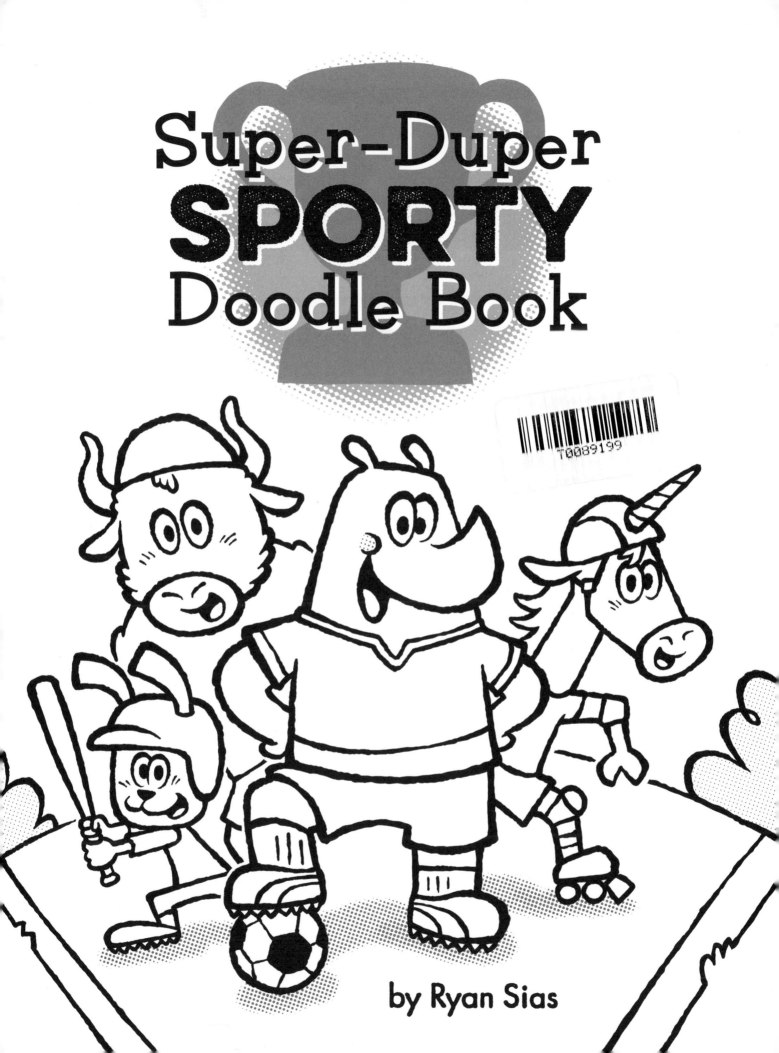

Super-Duper SPORTY Doodle Book

by Ryan Sias

Thanks to my wife, Hiroko, for giving me
joy, ideas, and loving support.

Text and illustrations copyright © 2019 by Ryan Sias

hmhco.com

The text of this book is set in Graham.
The display type was set in Plumbsky and Eveleth Dot.

ISBN: 978-1-328-80900-1

Manufactured in China
SCP 10 9 8 7 6 5 4 3 2 1
4500746914

This is Peter Parrot reporting live from Safari Stadium. Welcome to the Wild Games! Join in on the fun by writing, doodling, and searching through hidden pictures! Don't forget to use the stickers at the back of the book. Let the doodling begin!

Hooray! It's Funny Hat Day at the stadium! Draw some funny hats on these fans!

HOW TO DRAW

Psst! I've hidden 20 water bottles throughout this book. Can you find them all?

3

Roxy is packing her bag for the soccer game. Draw what she puts in her bag.

Roxy warms up with a soccer
ball. Color this ball with lots
of sporty colors.

Roxy Rhino

Draw your own.

Score a goal! Draw Roxy Rhino
dribbling to the net.

Oliver the Octopus is ready to defend the goal. Draw eight arms to block the kick.

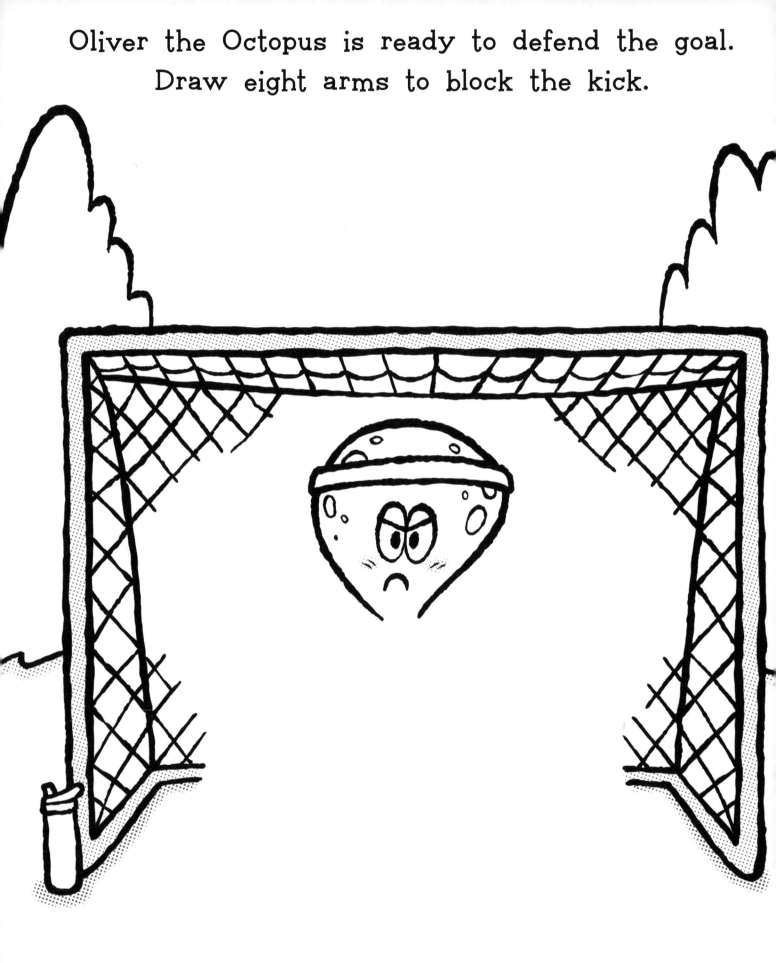

  Give him goalie gloves.

Story Starter

Sophia the Snake wants to play soccer with Roxy, but Roxy is scared of snakes. How do they become friends and play? Write a story!

Buttercup the Bulldog

Draw your own.

Draw Buttercup grinding the handrail on her skateboard.

BONUS! Draw a picture on her shirt.

Buttercup likes monsters.
Draw a monster on her skateboard.

BONUS! What's the name of the monster? Write it in fancy letters on her skateboard!

Buttercup does a huge ollie on the ramp and jumps over something tall. What does Buttercup jump over? Draw it!

Buttercup is hungry from all that skating.
Draw her favorite pizza topping!

paintbrush

flag

jump rope

rocket

football

book

windsurfing board

roller skate

magnifying glass

mug

Kala the Kangaroo

Draw your own.

Draw Kala doing a slam dunk!

BONUS! Kala dunks so hard that it breaks the backboard. Draw a crack in the backboard.

The shot blocker on the
other team is very tall.
Draw her!

Kala is showing how she can spin many basketballs at once. Draw basketballs spinning on her finger, foot, tail, and head.

Make Kala's sneakers look super cool!

Kara the Koala and Billy the Bilby want to do a slam dunk. How can they work together to make it happen?

Brett the Beaver

Draw your own.

One more player is needed for
the bowling team. Draw him.

Brett the Beaver gets a new bowling ball with flames on it. Decorate Brett's bowling ball.

BONUS! Add more bowling balls on the rack.

Brett got hungry and ate all the bowling pins! Draw something to replace the pins.

Brett is crying because he got *another* gutter ball. What does Sparkles the Unicorn give him to cheer him up?

Find and Color the Hidden Items

27

Walter the Walrus is ready to
go windsurfing. Draw a sail
that has fish on it.

What does Walter see in the water?

Oh no! A storm is coming.
Draw dark clouds and lightning.

  Draw a big wave for Walter to surf on.

Story Starter

Walter finds someone stranded on a deserted island. What does he do next? Write a story!

Rick the Rabbit

Draw your own.

BONUS! Draw your own baseball.

It's Rick's turn at bat. Draw him.

Draw an animal that you think would make a great pitcher.

Give Mike the Mouse a huge
baseball glove to catch the
fly ball.

After Mike caught the ball, a fan asked him to sign it. What does his signature look like?

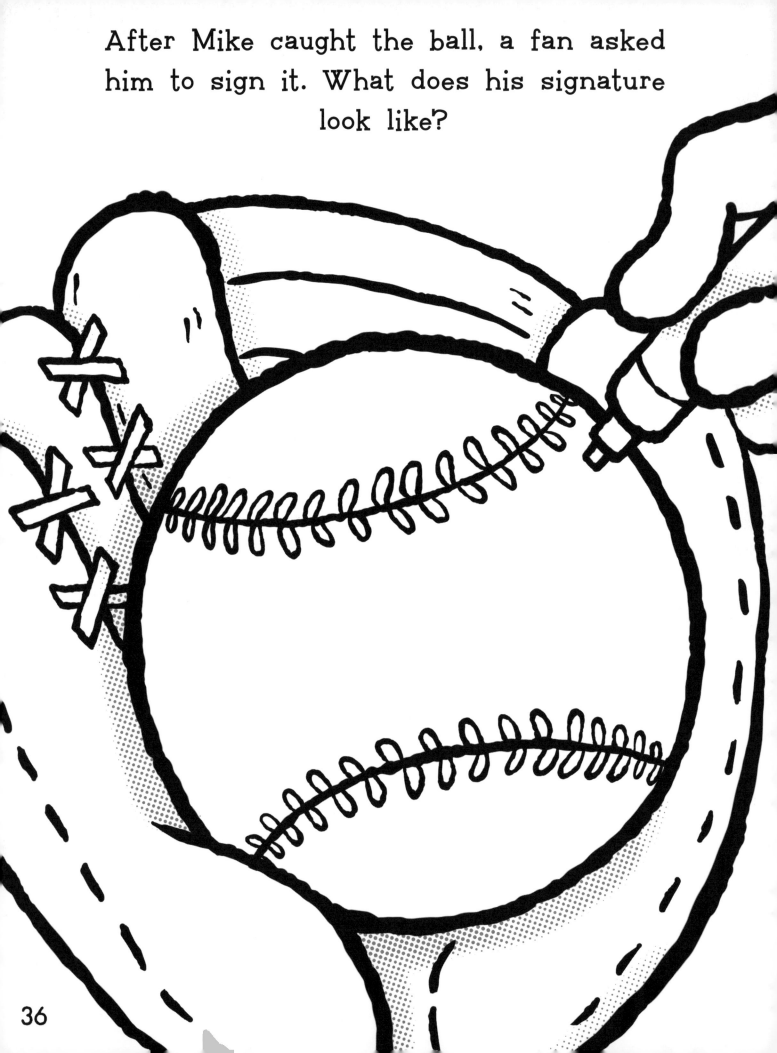

Steve the Shark

Draw your own.

BONUS! Draw Harry the Hammerhead diving for the volleyball.

Draw your own.

Draw Steve spiking the volleyball over the net. Draw Harry on the other side of the net diving in the sand for the ball.

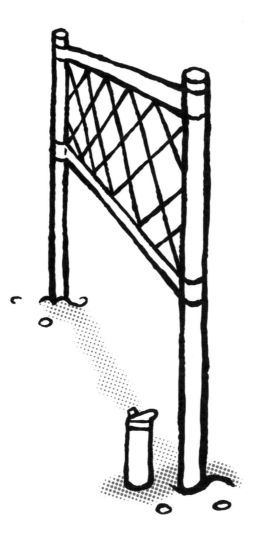

The volleyball is out of bounds,
Zed the Zebra referee blows his whistle.
Draw it!

Steve has a volleyball tattoo. Draw it!

Give Harry cool sunglasses.

42 **BONUS!** Color his shirt.

Story Starter

Oh no! The volleyball has popped on Steve's tooth. What does his team do? Write a story!

Puck the Poodle

Draw your own.

Draw Puck serving the tennis ball.

Uh-oh! Puck got a goofy doubles partner.
Draw his silly teammate.

Puck made a high-tech tennis racket. Draw it.

The tennis ball machine is out of control. It's lobbing too many balls at Puck. Fill the machine with as many tennis balls as you can.

BONUS! Draw lots of tennis balls flying toward Puck.

karate belt

basketball hoop

horseshoe

sneaker

whistle

kite

flag

ski

tent

ladder

49

It's time for Hailey the Hippo to throw the shot put. Draw something heavy for her to throw.

Hailey is an archery master. Draw her arrows in the center of the target.

Hailey's sneakers are super smelly after the 800 meter race. Draw stink lines to make them look smelly!

Story Starter

Oh no! Hailey is stuck at the top of the pole vault. She's scared! What happens next? Write a story.

Buck the Bear

Draw your own.

Draw Buck the Bear
scoring a goal with a slap
shot against Gina the Giraffe.

Ha-ha! The mascot replaced the hockey puck with something silly.
Draw it!

Break time! Draw a lightning bolt
on the Zamboni. Color it in.

The Bears won the game and the Pigs lost.
Draw the expressions on their faces.

Find and Color the Hidden Items

baseball bat   horseshoe   banana   crayon

mug

bread   flag   skateboard   candle   toothbrush

Draw your own.

BONUS! Draw a rainbow behind Sparkles.

Draw Sparkles jamming through
the pack of Wolf blockers.

Give Sparkles kneepads, elbow pads, and a helmet.

BONUS! Draw zany socks, face paint, and a colorful mouthguard.

Zed the Zebra referee sent two
Wolf blockers to the penalty box.
Draw their expressions.

Sparkles won MVP!
Draw the roller skate trophy!

Story Starter

Fred the Frog

Draw your own.

Draw Fred throwing the winning touchdown.

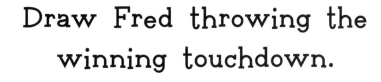

Draw the helmet design
for the Furious Frogs.

Oh no! Fred was tackled.
Draw a pile of football players
on top of him.

The football flies high in the air. Fred catches it with his tongue. Draw his tongue.

Fred scores a touchdown.
Draw him doing his funny
touchdown dance.

These fans used body paint to celebrate their favorite team. Draw designs all over them!

BONUS! Give them silly wigs.

Find and Color the Hidden Items

glove

baseball hat

baseball

hockey stick

bowling pin

bread

ring

bow and arrow

sneaker

bendy straw

Stacy the Sloth

Draw your own.

Stacy the Sloth is learning yoga.
Copy the pose from her teacher.

Stacy is learning mindfulness. Draw someplace peaceful for Stacy to meditate.

  Give Stacy a colorful yoga mat.

Story Starter

Stacy is writing a thankfulness list. What would you put on your thankfulness list?

Allie Gator

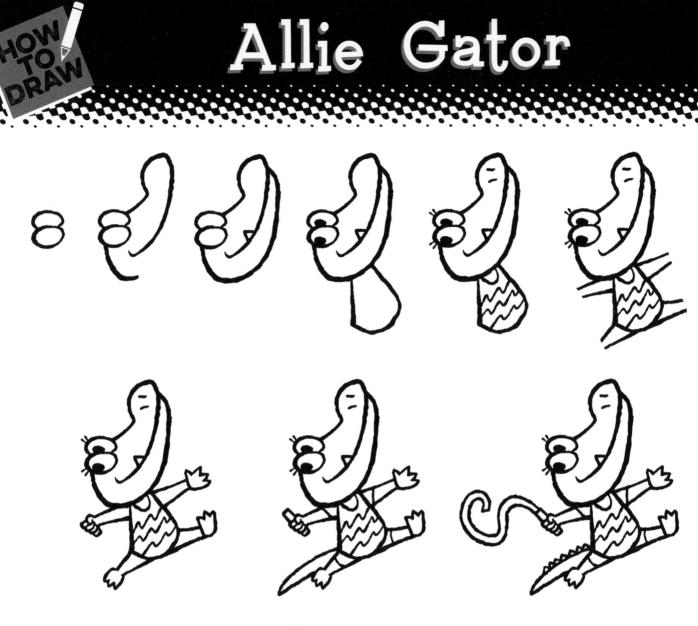

Draw your own.

Draw Allie Gator doing a giant gymnastics leap during her awesome floor routine.

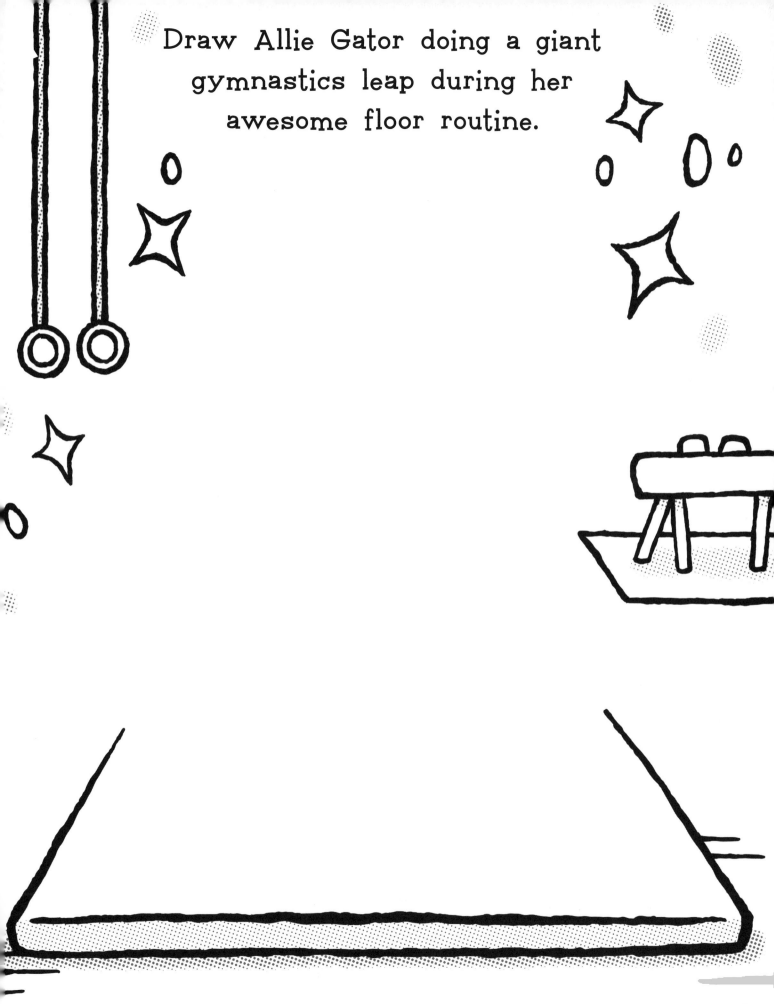

Draw Allie balancing on a very narrow balance beam.

Find and Color the Hidden Items

ring
dumbbell
boxing glove
hockey stick
carrot
home plate
book
rolling pin
comb
bell

Bruce the Buffalo

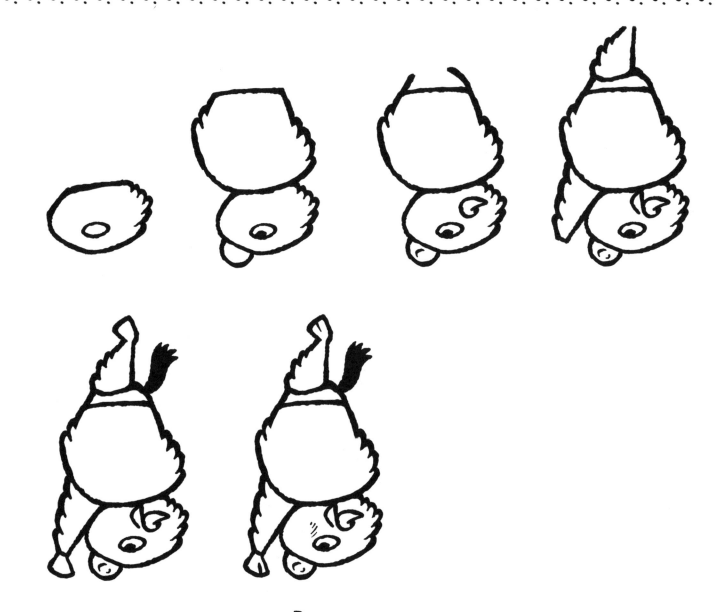

Draw your own.

Draw Bruce diving into the pool.

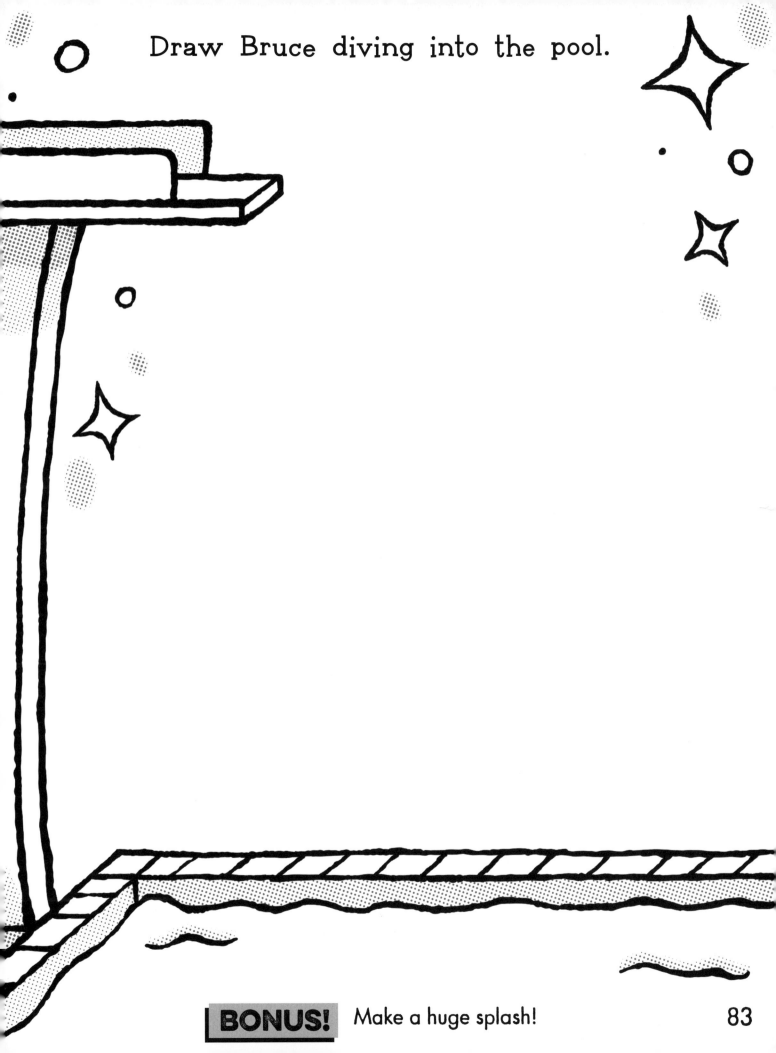

BONUS! Make a huge splash!

Bruce is getting ready to dive.
Draw a design on his
swimming cap!

BONUS! Draw swimming goggles on Bruce.

Story Starter

Bruce is nervous about the dive. How does he relax and get his head into the game? Write a story!

Belle the Baboon

Draw your own.

Draw Belle leading
the bicycle race!

Oh no! There's a huge hill to pedal up. Draw it!

  **BONUS!** Put a twisty bike path on the hill for Belle to follow.

Find and Color the Hidden Items

slice of pie

snake

whistle

ruler

cane

crown

badminton birdie

catcher's mitt

sailboat

golf ball and tee

It's a parade for the winners
of the Wild Games.
Draw the fancy
car that is carrying them.

BONUS! Add balloons to the car.

Draw a giant float for your favorite team.

 Fill the sky with balloons and confetti.

It's awards time! Give Buck a hockey
trophy and hang a medal around
Hailey's neck!

Puck gets a fancy plate for his tennis win. Fred wins a football trophy bigger than his whole body. Buttercup wins a skateboard trophy for biggest vertical jump. Draw them.

It's been a great day at the Wild Games.
Everyone enjoys the festive fireworks.
Draw sports-shaped fireworks in the sky!

Fun was had by all.
Draw smiley face fireworks!

Did you find all the water bottles? Keep track by coloring in the page numbers where you've found them.

Hint: Corresponding page numbers are in the center of the water bottles.

4 8 11 19 21 34 39 43 46 50

57 62 63 72 75 80 85 87 91 95

p.15

Find and Color the Hidden Items

p. 27

Find and Color the Hidden Items

p. 37

Find and Color the Hidden Items

p. 49

Find and Color the Hidden Items

p. 59

Find and Color the Hidden Items

p. 73

Find and Color the Hidden Items

p. 81

Find and Color the Hidden Items

p. 89

Find and Color the Hidden Items

This is Peter Parrot signing off from the Wild Games at Safari Stadium! Great job drawing, doodling, stickering, and writing. Keep on drawing!

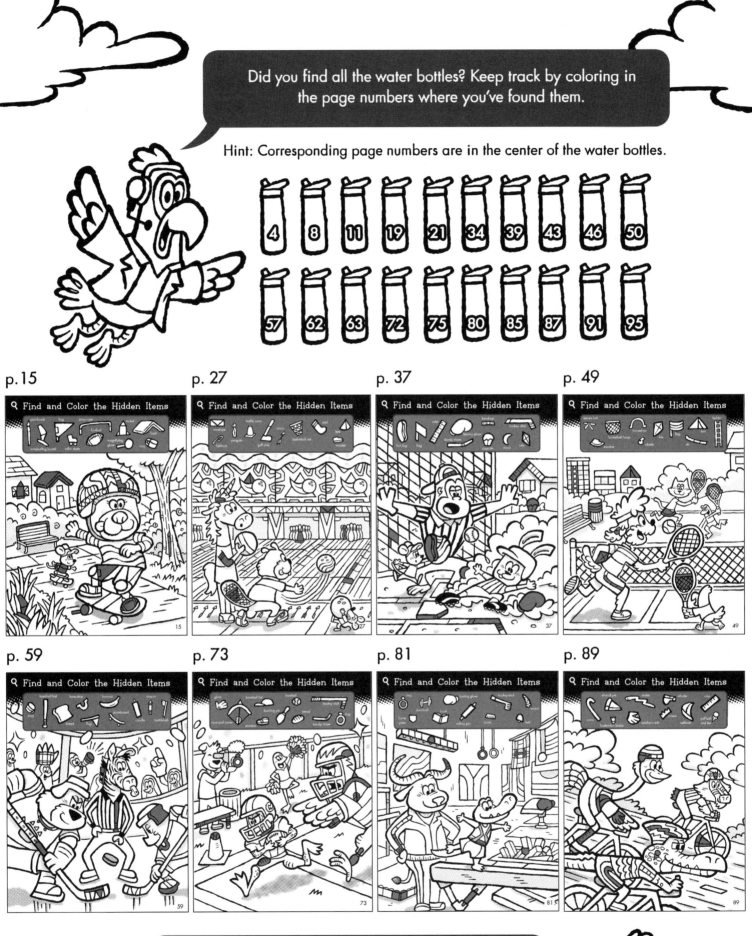